D1334956

# Workplace Survival

### Maintaining Faith Through Life's Catastrophes

by

Dorothy Ferrell

authorHOUSE®

*AuthorHouse™*
*1663 Liberty Drive, Suite 200*
*Bloomington, IN 47403*
*www.authorhouse.com*
*Phone: 1-800-839-8640*

*First published by AuthorHouse 10/8/2007*

*ISBN: 978-1-4343-2058-2 (sc)*

*Printed in the United States of America*
*Bloomington, Indiana*
*This book is printed on acid-free paper.*

*Unless otherwise indicated, all scripture quotations are from the*
*King James version of the Bible. Scripture references are taken from*
*Holman Bible Publishers, Copyright 1998. Used by permission.*
*Library of Congress Control Number: 2007906953*

# DEDICATION

This book would not have been possible if it was not for almighty God who is number one in my life. My daily reading of the number one best seller, *The Bible*, written by my favorite author, "God." For it was God's love and mercy that gave me a second chance at life to be able to share my testimony in this book with others. I say, thank you, God.

To my mom and dad for being my parents and for spending fifty-six years together until death parted them. Dad passed away on February 12, 2000. He was my father and best friend. When the year 2006 began, just when I thought my life was coming together—eight days into January—my mom got sick and passed away suddenly from pneumonia. She was my mother and best girlfriend. They are gone, but will forever remain in my heart.

To my three children, Shonna, Jerald, and Jennifer; my daughter-in-law Reneka, son-in-law William and my three grandsons, Devin, David, and Jalen and my two granddaughters Jeryn AnnMarie, and Jeila Marie. And to grandbaby number six Jeremiah. I love you all and thank God for giving me a wonderful family.

To my sisters Ruby and Marguerita, and my brother-in-law Fred, thank you for all your help during my hardships and for being there for me. To all the rest of family, my two brothers, sister-in-law and a host of nieces and nephews and great nieces and nephews, thank you for being my family.

I say a special thank you to the following men and women of God: For Dr. Morris Cerullo for twenty years of his teachings. The wisdom he has poured into my life only God can give, and all the money in the world could not buy God's wisdom. You could not put a cost on the teachings I have received from this true servant of God. To my Pastor, Bishop Jakes for ministering the word of God which helped to encourage my faith through the darkest times in my life through your Bible teachings, and for being a coach and a mentor to pull out of me what I never knew was inside—like starting a ministry and writing a book. To Mrs. Serita Jakes whose words of encouragement spoken at our PHIPA meetings, which helped build my faith as God's leading lady. To Bishop Staples Internet teachings and preaching the word of God during this season taught me how to praise my way out of my circumstances, even when I didn't feel like it, I say thank you.

A special thank you to Pastor Donna Bartram, the woman who taught me what intercession was all about and for all her prayers, girl-to-girl talks, and her teachings. I can never forget all the wonderful meetings we had together, God bless you, Donna. To the "Wailing California Women" prayer warriors and intercessors, Bea, Audrey, Josie, Carolyn, and Joanne who stood with me in prayer during the horrific storm.

To my attorneys and my doctor, thank God for giving me the right people who helped me get through victoriously. To three of my former co-workers, thank you for your encouragement.

To the Agreed Medical Examiner (AME) after giving me five hours of strenuous pulmonary testing, and who wrote the truth in his report based on the results of the tests. Thank you for your integrity and standing for truth in these last days where right is wrong and wrong is right.

Last but not least, the seven close family members who passed away since the beginning of 2000, which included my dad, February 2000, and the last six from 2004-2006, Mom, John, Ann, Roy, Uncle Billie, and Big John, I thank God for their lives and for the years we had together. When you lose your health, your job, finances, your loved ones back-to-back, and three grandchildren being born and ending up in neonatal intensive care for two to three months fighting for their lives, it's very hard. (In 1999, my second grandson, little David, had a 1 percent chance of survival, but beat the odds. He was diagnosed with a mild case of cerebral palsy, but I'm believing God that he will be totally healed one day).

Then in 2004 another grandson with a 50 percent chance of survival; 2006 a granddaughter born premature, but all are alive and well, thanks to the good Lord. When I look back, I know the only way I made it was through my faith in God and trying my best to stay FOCUSED.

Love,

Dot

# WORKPLACE SURVIVAL

In 2005, I was diagnosed with "Chronic Obstruction Pulmonary Disease." I never had asthma, nor allergies and I never smoked, but I went to work healthy and ended up sick with lung disease. In a 1999 air quality report, it said that the internal appearance of the air-handling units appeared to be "in generally poor condition with many items requiring attention." But three years passed before any renovation work was done.

I'm writing this book to be an encouragement to others who read it that they may realize the dangers of working in a sick building, better known as Sick Building Syndrome. This is also for those who may be going through something similar, or who may have friends and family who have experienced injury due to a sick building or any injury where they were violated. You may be in a very dark season of your life. Your storm of life may not be a "sick building" but I want to let you know, never give up.

After fourteen-and one-half years of employment with this government, I ended my career overnight due to "recklessness." It all started with the installation of a heating, ventilation and air conditioning unit (HVAC) in a 1960s vintage anemic building. Many dangerous toxins were known to be in the building—lead, aluminum, chromium, asbestos, mold, dust, fiber, fungus and God only knows what else. The recklessness caused the dangerous poisons to come through the overhead vents in my office and into my airways and lungs that were injured.

The asbestos had been located in the basement and the second floor where I worked. They had to be removed before the HVAC could be installed. My employer spent one million dollars for a new unit, but the forty-year-old ducts were not replaced.

I survived to share with others my true story of this unreal ordeal. In my case, a human resources/risk management department knew that this building was too sick to even undertake such a renovation project. Employees were not relocated to other buildings during this process, but were made to believe that everything was going fine.

In 2004, the governor of my state issued a reform to the workers compensation laws. In watching a video about workers compensation, I learned that the fine for fraudulent claims is five years in jail or $50,000. It also stated that workers not adhering to safety rules caused 95 percent of the injuries, and then there was the 5 percent, which were caused by the employer. The injury that you are about to read happened to me and put me into the 5 percent category—the injury was caused by the negligence of my employer.

# CONTENTS

# PART 1

# WORK BEGINNINGS

I was born and raised in southern California. I worked for other government entities and also private corporations that had integrity and good employer/employee relations. People had job ethics; I know the time which we live in now has changed drastically. I can only speak for the region of the country where I was born and raised. I see the integrity and job ethics being thrown out of the workplace by many once-good employers who had hired leaders that compromised their work ethics and they have a "right is wrong and wrong is right" attitude.

In the 80s, I worked in the aerospace industry, which was very big in southern California. However, in the decade of the 90s, the industry began to move out of California and moved to other states. I worked on the B2 bomber for an aerospace company, which was one of the best jobs of my life. Nevertheless, all good things ended after six years. The cutbacks began and I was laid off in 1989.

Being a Christian, the Bible is my roadmap to life. When my grandsons came over to spend the weekend, they would love for me to read the Bible story about David and Goliath. It was about this little boy David who had a "slingshot and some stones," and he slew the big giant Goliath. In my story, I equate myself to David and my former employer to Goliath.

My employment with this city government began in 1990. I was hired in the redevelopment department as a senior administrative secretary for the director. I was told this city government was a highly political city—more than the surrounding cities. I didn't really know what politics were, except that you voted for the best person who you thought would do a good job in representing the people. This was all I knew about politics. I didn't know what goes on behind closed doors in the political arena until my journey with this government. I had been laid off from my former employer, and I needed a job to help my husband pay the mortgage, bills, and to keep a roof over our heads and raise our three children.

My first two years were great, but after that, I began to see what "politics" were—a roller coaster ride. On any job you will encounter problems, which is normal. During my tenure of employment, I met a lot of beautiful employees, elected officials and good men and women in the city government. However, there is always the other side of the coin. A few bad apples can be wrongfully placed into leadership positions and will compromise to keep their jobs. As the old saying goes, "It's not what you know, but who you know." When it became too political for me, I looked for another job—like most Americans who get tired—but to no avail.

# PART 2

# TRANSFER TO THE POLICE BUILDING

I worked for nine months in the administration office, which was comprised of the mayor, city council, and city administrator offices. Then I was transferred in July 2001 to the police department. I was assigned as a senior administrative assistant to work for the police chief as his right hand.

I was an honest and truthful person and I didn't know how to play politics to keep my job in the oval office. I hadn't done anything wrong; I just didn't fit in with politics. The city hall management and police department were not the best of friends, so they figured I would fit in with the police, which I did.

Working for the police was the best three years for me. I didn't have people looking over my shoulder, lying on me, hiding my files, and going through my computer. I didn't have to do two or three jobs and only get paid for one. The big problem with the police department was the old building, which had not been taken care of over the years. In reality, the building needed to be condemned.

I went to work daily, ate the right foods, drank plenty of water, and walked two miles five days a week. I saw my doctor regularly for checkups and I was in great health for a person over fifty. My work schedule was a 4/10 shift—four days a week, Monday through Thursday, ten hours a day, and off Fridays, Saturdays and Sundays.

In 2001, I started a non-profit ministry with the state of California, which reached out to lost and hurting people. My ministry did outreaches that involved feeding and clothing the homeless, and volunteering at a homeless mother's and little children's shelter. I volunteered one Saturday a month to teach God's word and minister to the homeless mothers and young children at the shelter. The goal was to help give these mothers hope that they could be something in life and that people were there to give them a hand. We had birthday parties for the children, Christmas parties, and mother's day for the mothers. I had a great time helping those who were less fortunate. I forgot my problems and myself when I saw the faces of those little children who lived in abuse, poverty, and God knows what else. I found out how rewarding it is to help others. It kept me busy on my days off—Friday, Saturday, and Sunday. Sundays were reserved for church services where we worshiped God, and I taught the Bible to those in attendance.

I also held quarterly prayer breakfasts at a local hotel, which was open to people all over the southern California area.

Once a year, I coordinated the National Day of Prayer, held on the first Thursday of May each year. It was for the city, and it was attended by the mayor and council, assembly, and senate members, also representatives and judges. Also in attendance were hundreds of citizens and employees throughout the city. Everyone joined in prayer for our nation. I also conducted prayer for the government on our lunch hour on Tuesdays with other civic center employees. We held Bible studies in the library on our lunch hour on Wednesdays for government employees for about ten years. One year, we prayed, and the crime rate went down in our city tremendously.

I enjoyed my job in the police department. In 2002, I was one of the top three candidates nominated for "Employee of the Year," which included candidates from local businesses, the school district, local and county government and colleges in a city with 150,000 residents.

In the three years I worked in the police department, I worked for four police chiefs. My first chief retired and one of the captains became acting chief for six weeks. Then he retired and an interim police chief came aboard to hold the police department together for five months. In April 2003, they hired a new police chief after conducting a nationwide recruitment. All four men were great to work for and treated me with the utmost respect.

In 2001, the city council began to look at another building for the police department, but it would take five years before anything came forth. This city was over 100 years old, so there was hardly any vacant land available in the downtown area unless a building was torn down and a new building built.

# PART 3

# The Beginning—Questions and Answers

My story starts somewhere in 2002. The police department had been experiencing ventilation problems in a 1963 vintage-aging ventilation system that was just about ready to take its last breath. There was a small group of police staff who were assigned to work with the city's risk management department in preparation for putting in a new heating, ventilation, and air-conditioning (HVAC) unit. The employees' first awareness of what was happening in the building began on June 13, 2002.

The employees of the police department received a memo on June 13, 2002 from the human resources/risk management director; "NOTICE TO ALL EMPLOYEES." The subject matter was "ASBESTOS IDENTIFICATION AND REMEDIATION NOTIFICATION (Assembly Bill 3713).

The memo stated that, "The city government will be performing an asbestos identification/removal/repair/clean-up project in several areas of the police department that have been found to contain asbestos building material." It named the four areas that had been found—one was on the second floor where I worked. "An approved and qualified contractor will be performing remediation work. The work is scheduled for June 20, 2002 through June 21, 2002, from 7:00 p.m. to 3:30 a.m.

The work areas will be isolated from other building areas." The memo said, "Refer any questions regarding this matter to the safety officer."

There were four unions that represented all the employees in the building. The employees became very concerned regarding this asbestos remediation. On June 17, 2002, the non-sworn employees—who spent their entire work shifts in the building—had the following concerns, which were sent to the safety officer by our union president. On June 18, 2002, the safety officer responded to the questions and a memo was placed on the bulletin board for all employees that said, "NOTICE TO OCCUPANTS OF THE POLICE DEPARTMENT" with the questions and answers to the following concerns:

> 1. While the asbestos is being removed, is it safe for personnel to be in the building? Yes. All areas where work will be conducted will be clearly marked and blocked off. A qualified, licensed asbestos removal contractor will conduct the work. Employees will not be allowed to enter these areas. Employees in areas not marked will be able to conduct normal work practices safely.
>
> 2. What measures will be taken to ensure asbestos particles will not be returned in the air-conditioning unit? There are a total of five air-handling units in the police department. Each unit supplies air to specific locations/ floors throughout the building. Because each unit operates independently, air particulates cannot travel from unit to unit. Therefore, the building operator will shut down a specific unit in an area where work is being done while the other air-handling units remain operating. In addition, to ensure there is no breaching of particles to the outside, all duct openings and doors will be sealed with duct tape in work areas prior to the start of work.

3. Should personnel who have respiratory sensitivity/ pregnant conditions be removed from the area?
No. All work areas will be sealed and isolated prior to start of work. Therefore, indoor air concentrations outside the work area will be the same as any other normal workday.

4. Will it be warm in areas where air-handling system are shut down?
Yes. One of the reasons we are conducting work at night is because it is cooler. In addition, fans will be available to employees during this project. If possible, employees should wear light clothing. In addition, drink plenty of water.

5. Will the employees be notified of the results of identification?
Assembly Bill 3713 states employers must inform employees of the location of asbestos containing material. In addition, the city will annually notify employees of asbestos locations and prior to any renovation/demolition work. Finally, asbestos awareness training is also available through the human resources department.

Again, we thank you for your cooperation and patience during this time. Please direct any questions regarding this matter to the safety officer.

On July 22, 2002, a memo went to the police chief from the safety officer to post on the bulletin board for the employees. It read, "NOTICE TO OCCUPANTS OF POLICE DEPARTMENT. Subject ASBESTOS IDENTIFICATION AND REMEDIATION NOTIFICATION (Assembly Bill 3713)."

The memo let the employees know that on June 20, 2002 the contractor removed, repaired, and cleaned up several areas as identified in the June 13, 2002 notice. The work was conducted in accordance with regulatory requirements.

This July 22, 2002 memo stated, "Forensic analytical collected a total of seven air samples from selected offices and above the ceiling tile on the second floor (this is where I worked) during the normal working business hours." It gave the sample results range and the Environmental Protection Agency (EPA's) limit for asbestos and the California Occupational Safety and Health Administration's (Cal/OSHA) limit. "The air sample with the highest result was submitted for further analysis that specifically identifies asbestos fibers."

This same memo also stated, "On June 24, 2002, forensic analytical conducted a survey of suspected asbestos and lead from the men's locker area located in the basement. The survey was conducted in anticipation of renovation activities. Sample results indicate asbestos containing material in the acoustical ceiling tile and pipe joint insulation." It also stated, "The percentage of lead in the wall of the beige paint and gray ceramic tile is greater than the current Cal/OSHA (Title 8 CCR 1532.1) lead volumes." Therefore, work performed on surfaces containing lead—including renovation, manual demolition, scraping, welding—will comply with this regulation.

The police department (PD) will be notified when renovation activities will begin in the regulated area and the safety precautions that will be taken during the period.

I was told and it was confirmed that the safety officer was terminated for sharing sensitive contamination figures with police staff working on the project. The risk manager was the safety officer's supervisor and did not want the police staff to know how high the lead figures were, which we later discovered were four to five times the EPA and Cal/OSHA requirements. In other words, my employer knew the dangerous risks in undertaking this project before they even started the abatement process. My employer gambled with not only my life, but also the lives over 300 employees by going forward with this project. In my opinion, it would have been wiser to remove as many employees as possible out of harms way, even if they had to put them in trailers or find another building.

Proverbs 29:8, *"Scornful men bring a city into a snare; but wise men turn away wrath."*

# PART 4

# THE NIGHTMARE BEGINS

The next memo to the employees was dated November 14, 2002 and was address to "All Personnel" from one of the sergeant's who worked on the project from inside the police department building. The memo's subject was, "Heating Ventilation Air Conditioning (HVAC) Project Asbestos Concerns." It let us know the energy contractor was going to begin the HVAC upgrade project on the next day, November 15, 2002.

The memo explained to the employees how "asbestos was used in the 60s as a fire retardant. The police building has asbestos sprayed on the building's actual ceilings. These asbestos surfaces are not visible because all work areas have "drop" ceilings, which hang several feet below the actual hard ceilings."

"Undisturbed asbestos-covered surfaces present no health hazard. However, when asbestos-covered surfaces are disturbed, asbestos particles become airborne. The particles at that time become a health hazard."

"The first phase of the contractor's work will address asbestos surfaces. Wherever the contractor is going to work in the ceilings, they must first "encapsule" the asbestos-covered surfaces, which involve spray coating the asbestos. Encapsuled asbestos presents no health hazard. If the encapsuled asbestos is disturbed, it breaks off from the ceiling as a solid clump that can be picked up and discarded. No airborne particles are created, or released."

"The contractor will encapsule all of the areas where they will be working in the ceiling. After the encapsuling, the contractor will vacuum all the encapsulated debris from the top of the "drop" ceilings, which are overhead. The encapsulated debris is not hazardous, but the vacuuming results in a cleaner work area. Finally, before declaring the second floor safe to resume work, the contractor will take air samples to ensure that no asbestos particle hazard exists."

"Upon return to work on Monday, November 18, 2002 (the second floor was closed off on Friday, Saturday and Sunday which were most of the employees' off days who worked on this floor), the visible plastic covers serve to provide a barrier in case the encapsuled asbestos falls (e.g. due to an earthquake). These plastic covers will remain in place until the work is completed in March 2003."

"If you have concerns about asbestos, please know that the contractor employees also recognize the potential dangers. The contractor utilizes the services of an asbestos expert subcontractor, to provide a safe environment for its own employees to work, as well as for you. The contractor and subcontractor employees will work in direct proximity to the asbestos-covered surfaces for several months. Their work this weekend is intended to insure that no asbestos hazard is created through the energy upgrade construction. Additionally, the contractor will take other readings throughout the duration of this project to insure a safe work environment for their employees, and for you."

"If you have any questions or concerns not addressed by this memorandum, please contact the sergeant."

# PART 5

# THE BOTCHED ASBESTOS ABATEMENT

On Monday morning, November 18, 2002, when I walked into my office on the second floor, panels in the ceiling were missing. In other offices on the second floor—the detective bureau—the plastic was hanging off the ceilings and on the floor in most areas. Work areas covered with plastic by the employees—prior to leaving the week before—were covered with a thin layer of white powdery residue of unknown content.

I quote one of the lieutenants who worked on the project and had to retire in December 2003 because he was also injured during the "reckless renovation." He said,

"The only description I can give of the visible work at this point is "slipshod" at best. If this work is representative of the level of quality control, exercised over other aspects of the project, then we may only assume many employees have already been unnecessarily exposed to a serious health threat. In fact, if the contractor is also providing the hazards safety quality assurance reports, I liken that to allowing the suspect in a criminal incident to collect and present their own evidence in a case."

The word "slipshod" according to Webster's dictionary is defined as "shabby, careless." It looked as though the contractor was so concerned about the workers (which they should have been) but they forgot about the employees who were going to walk right back into a Monday morning nightmare. Not everything that was supposed to be done to take precautionary measures was done. The encapsuling and vacuuming of the debris was not done.

Proverbs 21:12, *"The righteous man wisely considereth the house of the wicked; but God overthroweth the wicked for their wickedness."*

After the botched job that was done by the so-called "asbestos experts," we reported the incident about the missing panels in our office. The facilities coordinator and one of the workmen ran upstairs and sealed the area off with plastic. Photos were even taken in the detective's bureau. It was unbelievable the work that had been done.

I worked in an office adjacent to the police chief, and I shared the office with the administrative assistant to one of the captains, whose office was adjacent to her.

My office ventilation system was at the end of a unit, so that meant we were breathing backed-up dust, debris, and toxins. At night, they would allow a percentage of outside air to come into the building, which is legal. The chief and the captain's office were not at the end of a vent, so they did not have the backup in their offices. When I and the other assistant would come to work, we would suddenly start coughing. In 2002, my co-worker and I began to cough and asked the safety officer if he could check our air quality. This is when they came over and checked the air quality. We didn't really know the results.

I don't remember exact dates; we both assumed it was maybe colds or flu since we were in fall and flu season, which is normally December and January.

The holiday season was coming up and most people took off. The administration offices were closed for two weeks at Christmas and then re-opened after New Years. This was a new law the city hall had instituted. You had to use your own vacation time. The police department never closes, so officers, dispatchers and records technicians work through scheduled shifts. It was pretty quiet concerning the HVAC unit during the holiday season, until the first of the year.

# PART 6

# Second Major Renovation Disaster

On the morning of February 27, 2003 at 8:30 a.m., I walked into the building and didn't know what was happening. The front desk, records, and the watch commander's office (which were all on the first floor) were filled with a tremendous amount of noxious smoke flowing from the overhead HVAC system vents. The smoke caused many employees to have labored breathing and watery eyes.

It turns out one of the workers working on the system in the basement of the police department had just used a torch to cut through the wall of a ventilation system plenum chamber—a space or all space every part of which is full of matter. It's a condition where the pressure of the air in an enclosed space is greater than that of the outside atmosphere, which resulted in smoke filling the first floor. The plenum chamber was forty-plus years old and had several layers of paint and insulation, which were vaporized in the cutting process. This was another major breach in the safety curtain.

The worker used a cutting torch instead of an electric saw to cut through sheet metal on the HVAC cabinet. The smoke and odor worked its way through the ventilation system. The contractor told our staff they should have shut the ventilation system off before working on it, which would have contained the smoke.

Earlier, I mentioned that heavy lead was already four to five times the Cal/OSHA limit and this had not been removed yet. Therefore, the worker was cutting through aluminum, chromium, iron and tin along with the lead. It's a wonder we all didn't die. I know some employees were sent to the doctor from the smoke that affected their respiratory system.

All the dangerous toxins they considered hazardous were fine until it was disturbed. From my vantage point—coming in and out of the building—everything was disturbed. Also, during the construction, dust, contaminates, and hazardous materials were to be properly contained to prevent any exposure to employees working in the building. This was not done.

The lives of the people were jeopardized again by "recklessness." Inside those walls where the torch went in were aluminum and chromium. Only God knows whatever we had all been exposed to. Only time would tell the damage to employees' health behind the "recklessness."

# PART 7

# COMPLAINTS FROM OTHER EMPLOYEES

In March 2003, employees on the second floor where I worked, began to complain about debris coming from the ducts. Some employees would come to work and find black soot on their desks. I know I constantly had to dust off my desk in order to work. We received the following memo on Tuesday, March 18, 2003, from the sergeant who was working on the program.

"I received a reply from the last memo to let me know some soot also fell from some second floor vents. Because of your (valid) concerns, I would like to give you some more information, which I hope will ease any concerns you may have by letting you know what steps we have taken."

"The second floor, as you know, received the bulk of attention during this HVAC. In fact, most of the new equipment is intended to remedy temperature problems here on the second floor that are not present in the basement or main floor."

"The existing air ducts in the building were not changed as part of this project. The ducts were found to be in suitable shape to carry the air. HOWEVER, we were made aware that during the forty-year existence of the building, some debris has built up in the ducts, which is simply something that happens naturally. We were also made aware that with the increased air flow of the new HVAC, some existing debris could be blown loose."

"In response, we did several things."

"First, we had an independent third party contractor collect debris from the ducts and ran tests, so we would know what the stuff is, IF it was blown loose. The tests indicated the presence of soot and very small amounts of fiberglass (NO asbestos), which can be irritants in large amounts, but no biological or chemical hazards."

"Second, we paid additional to have a subcontractor come in and clean as much of the ducting as could be reached, just as a precaution to remove as much as possible."

"Third, we requested filters to be put in over the registers (vents)—again, just as a precaution to catch any material blown loose during construction and testing. We removed the filters two weeks ago, thinking they would not be necessary, but with the latest incident (and your reports), we will have new filters put in, and kept in for months as a precaution. The exit vents aren't built to accommodate filters (think of your own systems at home), but we're putting them in anyway."

"Fourth, we had the third-party contractor run air quality tests on three different occasions to confirm that any level of particles in the air (because there are always some) was within allowable levels, and that any particles were not hazardous."

"Now, with all of that said, I still cannot provide you guarantees. As long as air blows through the ducts, there will always be some small amount of particles that are blown loose through the vents. But, I do hope to assure you that the administrative services division of the police department has taken and will continue to take any steps necessary to minimize inconvenience, and to eliminate hazards, and that I will respond to your concerns."

By this time, all four unions that represented the police department employees were asking the risk manager for her help in holding the contractor and vendors accountable for the promised control of hazardous materials present during the retrofitting of the HVAC system.

The risk manager's response to this second "recklessness" was, "While I share in your concerns, there's nothing we can do after the fact. Once an exposure occurs, there is no way to sample the air. All we can do is speculate the risk based on the materials involved. There is nothing more to do with regards to this incident."

# PART 8

# 2004—My Year of Personal Life Tragedies and Problems

This year started off with two family members' deaths—my mother-in-law, three days later my former husband, John, whom I spent over twenty years with. I always learned that you never take your personal problems to work, so I took off a week to grieve with my children. It was very difficult, but I had to be strong, which was hard.

In the same month, I had a condo in escrow that closed. I moved out of the family home where my husband and I had reared three children. After the deaths, I turned our home over to a reliable property management company to rent out until I could decide what I wanted to do with the property.

This company had a good reputation and they had been in business for over twenty years. I thought everything would work out well. To my surprise, somehow, one of his agents rented the property to a couple who had two sons, ages sixteen and twenty. The man was ill when they moved in and the first week he was rushed to the hospital where he passed away. The property management company tried to convince me that the boys were good boys.

After the first couple of weeks, my former neighbors called me every night. The boys were selling drugs out of my rental home. It was a large beautiful home that was built in late 1989. Thousands of dollars of upgrades were spent in 2003 on the property. The tenants had turned it into a hotel. A known prostitute was visiting the house daily. Here I am, a God-fearing woman with drug dealers, prostitutes, gang-bangers, and everything else going on in my rental property.

I told the neighbors to call the police whenever they saw suspicious activities so we could have a list of police calls that would help evict the tenants. This was unbelievable. The property management president told me in twenty years of business, they never had anything happen like this, and it would be difficult to get them out. I told him he put them in, and I wanted them out. After fighting with him to do his job, we were able to retrieve police calls and turn them over to an attorney who had them out in thirty days without my property being torn up. I was so sick during this time, and yet I had this burden added to everything else.

I took my home back, and put an ad in the paper. A nice Christian woman with three children and her mother rented it. They were very quiet and the neighbors liked them, so I was pleased.

To put injury onto insult, on May 19, 2004, I got a phone call that most grandparents look forward to—the birth of my third grandchild. After the two family members' deaths—three days apart, two months prior—I was looking forward to a new life. This was my oldest daughter's third child. I was in the delivery room, and for the first time, I cut the umbilical cord. It was a beautiful little baby boy, born full-term. My daughter had been sedated with medicine they had given her, so I walked with the nurse to the incubator where the nurse laid the baby down. One second later, his hand went limp, and he stopped breathing. I couldn't believe it. The doctors and nurses rushed in. Six hours later, his little incubator was loaded into a helicopter and taken on a fifty-minute ride to Kaiser Permanente's Neonatal Intensive care unit in Los Angeles, where the specialists were waiting for him. He was given a 50 percent chance to survive. I cried like a baby in the hallway by myself. I couldn't understand why God was allowing me to go through this. I felt like everyone in my family was being wiped out and I couldn't stop coughing.

My grandson was born with a hole in his diaphragm, which is called a diaphragmic hernia. It pushed his little organs over his lungs and cut off his breathing. The specialists were able to do surgery twice. They went in and pushed the little organs back in place successfully.

To make a long story short, after being in the hospital for two months, and enduring two surgeries, he is a strong and healthy little boy who gets into everything.

# PART 9

# Warning Signs of a Sick Building

I went back to work after being off a few days. My co-worker was still coughing and I started coughing all over again. It seemed that every time we would leave the building and get into our cars with the air-conditioning on, the coughing would stop. The coughing began to escalate by 2004. My co-worker and I became very suspicious about the building. Other employees in the building were having issues also.

We knew this was not a cold or flu. This was a "sick building problem" which was making us sick. Therefore, I went to my health care provider. My regular doctor was out so I saw another doctor. He examined my lungs and asked me if I had asthma. I told him no, I never had asthma nor any allergy problems. He said he heard wheezing in my lungs and he gave me breathing medication that asthma patients take. I took off a couple of days and returned to work. My co-worker got sick a week later. We both filed a worker's compensations claim with our employer by the later part of June 2004. Our claims were denied ninety days later.

I was told there was a web site for "Sick Building Syndrome" (SBS), which described situations in which building occupants experienced acute health and discomforts that appeared to be linked to time spent in a building, but no specific illness could be identified. The complaints may be localized in a particular room or zone, or may be widespread throughout the building. In contrast, the term "building related illness"

(BRI) is used when symptoms of a diagnosable illness are identified and can be attributed directly to the airborne building contaminants.

The report states, "A 1984 World Health Organization Committee report suggested that up to 30 percent of new and remodeled buildings worldwide may be the subject of excessive complaints related to indoor air quality (IAQ). Often the condition is temporary, but some buildings have long-term problems. Frequently, problems result when a building is operated or maintained in a manner that is inconsistent with its original design or prescribed procedures. Sometimes indoor air problems are a result of poor building design or occupant activities."

"Indicators of SBS include building occupants complaining of symptoms associated with acute discomfort. Examples are irritated eyes, runny nose, nasal congestion, scratchy throat, coughing, rashes, fever, nausea, headaches, dizziness, confusion, fatigue, difficulty in concentrating, and sensitive to odors."

Now without a doubt, I knew this was definitely a sick building that I had been working in. In a 1999 air quality report, it stated the building had "poor air handlers" and basically the building had not been taken care of.

By June 2004, my doctors had instructed me three times to take off from work. When I went to see my regular doctor, he put me on steroids, but my breathing was becoming worse. I was getting very fatigued and weak. My co-worker in the same office had the same symptoms, but mine were worse.

I told my chief that my co-worker and I were experiencing upper respiratory problems for the last six months and we thought it was due to the ventilation. There was definitely something coming through the vents which was making us sick, but we didn't know what it was. The safety officer was contacted regarding the matter. He, in turn, contacted an environmental company to come out and check the air quality.

At my home one evening, I was in prayer and worship before the Lord when I heard a "still small audible voice" say, "**Do not go back in the old building, or you will be dead in six months. Toxins are subtly coming through the vents over your head.**" I was scared to death, but I knew it was the Lord speaking to me, and warning me before destruction. I got so sick that I couldn't go back. My doctor took me out of the building and I obeyed God and never returned to the "old building."

Six months later, a pulmonary specialist said if I had gone back into the old building, my airways would have shut down. I would have suffocated to death. However, thanks to the good Lord, he didn't allow it.

PART 10

# Medical Leave

On July 22, 2004, when I went to the doctor, he would not allow me to go back in the building. He said my respiratory problems were coming from my environment (the old police building) and that I was a mystery.

I became so weak and short of breath that I could barely go up the stairs in my home. After pulmonary testing and allergy testing began on my body, my doctors found there was an obstruction over my airways, which was only allowing me to take 60 percent of air into my lungs. I would have literally suffocated and died if I had gone back into the building.

My first close encounter with death occurred a few days after I was taken off my job. In July, I was driving home from the store when I became very lightheaded. I felt like I was getting ready to stop breathing. It was frightening. My airways were closing, but I didn't know what it was. I remember stopping the car and calling, "JESUS" very loud, and then I got quiet. All of a sudden, breath came back into my body. I didn't drive my car for two months after that episode. I would cry at night so hard, asking God why I had to suffer like this. I felt like I had done something wrong in my life and I was being punished. I know it rains on the just and the unjust. In this life, we all will go through trials to help us grow stronger in Christ.

After having a husband, children, grandchildren and dogs, it was all over—no husband, and the children were all grown. My youngest was in college and staying with friends. I gave the dog away before I moved. I was learning how to live by myself and sick at the same time. For twenty-six years I was taking care of a family, but now I was alone and afraid. I didn't know what was happening to me and I didn't know how to take care of myself. I didn't know if I would live or die, and I was afraid. My whole life had taken a drastic turn. Nothing in my life made sense anymore.

I had to stop the ministry, but I had four close friends who kept in touch and prayed for me. However, everyone had his or her own busy lives to live. My children were going through the grief with the death of their father and grandmother. My oldest daughter was adjusting to the new baby being home and watching him to be sure he didn't get sick. My brother-in-law had just gone into hospice. My sister had retired from her job to take care of him during his last few months. He passed away in late October 2004. This was the third family death in eight months.

I would wake up about one o'clock in the morning and turn on Christian TV. There was a show that came on called Creation Scenes, and it showed nothing but beautiful scenes of waterfalls, the oceans, the mountains, and all of God's beautiful creations. There were Bible scriptures that were written on the screen which were very comforting. I remember one night it felt as if GOD was talking to me.

Jeremiah 30:17 came across the screen. *"I will restore health to thee, and heal thee of thy wounds saith the Lord."*—the wound meaning the injury.

I began to read my Bible more. I watched Christian TV more, and I listened to the word being taught on DVD. I would saturate my home with praise and worship music and this helped me. I couldn't go anywhere, except to see the worker's comp doctor, which the city scheduled me for my first visit on August 18, 2004. The total trip was over 200 miles. I had the city send a driver to take me, because I had stopped driving after my first "suffocation attack" in July 2004.

I had used all my sick leave, so I applied for "catastrophic"—this is when your co-workers who have over 300 sick-leave hours can donate increments of eight hours to you. I had hours donated which lasted six weeks—a blessing from the beautiful co-workers who helped me survive.

With the poor ventilation in the old building and the reckless renovation, the building was already suffering from SBS before I went to work there in 2001. Complaints were made to Cal/OSHA and I called to file a complaint regarding the "unsafe work environment" in the building. They fined the city at one point behind the old building and that was it.

By the beginning of August 2004, I was too sick and weak to handle my worker's compensation claim that I had filed. I was referred to a worker's compensation attorney in southern California that deals with law enforcement for sworn and non-sworn government employees. My attorney handled the sworn officers, but he took my case. I am forever grateful for this man hearing the cries of a non-sworn employee, and he didn't turn me down for help. The injury was a different kind of injury caused by a "sick building." It was not a common injury where if I fell down on the job and broke an arm or leg that you could visibly see an injury. I had an internal injury caused by a sick building and not many attorneys want to deal with a sick building case.

On August 6 and August 10, 2004, my doctor scheduled me for pulmonary and allergy tests. The allergy tests came back negative twice. Then they ran a blood test which proved negative. The pulmonary tests showed the "restriction or obstruction" over my airways and the 60 percent air capacity in my lungs.

On August 18, 2004, I was sent to an internal medicine doctor in the city of Orange. My regular doctor told me to take the results of the pulmonary tests he had administered so the internist could see what was happening to my lungs. The city's worker's compensation doctor ran a blood test, put a stethoscope to my lungs, and that was it. He didn't even take any internal lung testing, and this doctor specialized in internal medicine.

My employer tried to force me to come back to work when I was "totally disabled" in September 2004. From the 2004 air quality reports sent to their doctor, he said from looking at the air quality reports and listening to my chest via a stereoscope, I was okay to go back to work. Frankly, neither the doctors nor the allergist knew what was happening to me. All my allergy tests came back negative. My lung tests showed a "restriction or an obstruction over my airways" stopping air from going into my lungs. My employer said I had allergies from living in the desert where my new condo was, which proved false. It was the old police building making me sick.

I was in the world of the worker's compensation system. This arena is comprised of doctors and lawyers. I believe most employers want to get the injured workers well and back into the work force. I believe most workers want to get well and go back to work. However, some employers "doctor shop," which is the term used for employers who look for doctors who they know will work in their favor—so they won't have to pay the injured worker by denying their claim or giving them minimum benefits. In other words, the doctor would write a nice report in the employer's favor.

The city was saying I had moved to the desert and was allergic to the desert. They were trying to say that I had asthma, which was not true. All the medical tests proved negative for asthma and allergies. They didn't know what was happening. The only thing they could call it was "Reactive Airway Disease." A few months later this was ruled out. They realized that Reactive Airway Disease is asthma, and asthmatic patients can take a full capacity of air into the lungs, but cannot expel air. I was the opposite; I could not take a full capacity of air into my lungs, but I could expel. My doctor said, "You're a mystery. We don't know what's happening to you, but we do know it's coming from your environment."

29

# PART II

# MY SON'S WEDDING

One of the happy times of my life was seeing my only son get married. My son got married on September 5, 2004 and he had a beautiful wedding overlooking a lake at one of the beautiful hotels here in southern California. I was so afraid that I would be too sick to attend, but I prayed to God. I was able to stay at the hotel where they were getting married the night before the wedding. I did fine in the midst of a summer heat wave. The wedding was at four o'clock and the lake was surrounded by a large hotel and businesses, which blocked the late afternoon sun from beaming down on the crowd.

He walked me down the aisle, and sat me in the front row. Then he went back for the procession. I gave my son a hug and kiss. In my heart, I was saying to him, "I release you, my, son to your new bride and new life. Be blessed." The wedding was beautiful and I made it through without getting sick.

After the wedding, I spent the night at my elderly mother's house in Los Angeles, which was during the Labor Day weekend. It was so hot and she lived in a home with no air-conditioning. She lives about twenty-five minutes east of the Pacific Ocean. It may be hot during the day, but usually by mid-afternoon, a breeze comes through from the ocean and cools the air temperature. On this particular evening, there was no breeze, and my little mom believed in fans and keeping the windows closed. This was the house my dad purchased for my family when I was five years old. It was an old Los Angeles home built with quality craftsmanship. I moved out of the Los Angeles area years ago and during the last sixteen years, I lived inland. The inland area is located near mountains and deserts in San Bernardino County so you need a central air-conditioning unit. The temperatures get into the 100s all summer. The neighborhood had changed in Los Angeles like most of your American inner cities, and it was no longer a nice safe neighborhood.

At 1:00 a.m., I woke up gasping for air. I felt another "suffocation attack" coming on. I opened the front door and began to breathe the fresh air. It woke my mom up and she wanted to call the Los Angeles fire department paramedics and ambulance. I told her no; I would be all right after I allowed the cool air to breathe on me and I begin to feel better. I know if the LAPD—L.A. fire department came, I would be rushed to some emergency room and allowed to sit on a gurney for hours. I would have probably died in the emergency room in a Los Angeles hospital with all the drama that goes on in the inner city.

By 2:30 a.m., I told my mom I had to leave. I couldn't take the heat in the house. Months later, I learned that people with Chronic Obstruction Pulmonary Disease had airways that began to close up when they were exposed to heat and humidity. I drove home with the air-conditioning on and my cell phone by my side. I made it safely home and went to sleep.

# PART 12

# Decision to Retire

On September 18, 2004, I had another exam with the same doctor, and he said the air quality tests showed the building was fine. I didn't know until over a year later that my employer only sent him the current 2004 air quality reports. More than a year later, I learned that the 2001, 2002, and 2003 air quality reports were missing. I found this out at my deposition in 2005.

I didn't know what was happening to me and I didn't want to share anything with my family for they might fear that I was going to die. It was a traumatic year for my family. Everyone was going through their own crisis, and so I suffered quietly. I knew my family loved me and would do anything to help, but it was too difficult to get them involved.

My move to the desert in March 2004 placed me about an hour-and-a-half drive from my mother, and the rest of my family. My dad passed away in 2000 after being married to my mom for fifty-six years. Two of my children were about forty-five minutes away, and the closest relative was my oldest daughter and grandsons who lived fifteen minutes away.

My father-in-law lived in Nevada and he was going through the grief of losing a wife and a son, three days a part. My friends prayed with me as I said, but they had their own problems. My co-worker would call me periodically or send me a little note, but she was still coughing and trying to hang in there, so I couldn't trouble her.

I found peace reading my Bible and Christian books, and watching Christian satellite TV (where there are about five stations). I would watch DVDs and videos that were funny and made me laugh. The Bible says laughter is medicine for the soul. I couldn't listen to the news; it was nothing but murder, violence, and nothing positive in southern California.

In late September 2004, I received three phones calls from my employer saying the city's doctor said it was okay for me to go back to work on Monday—three days away. I never received an official letter stating this. My doctor had filed out their "Physician or Practitioner Certification—Employee Serious Health Condition" on August 5, 2004 with a return date as "pending."

I had to use common sense and make a decision. I knew I was too sick to go back to work and it would be detrimental for me if I returned. I knew if I didn't show up to work in three days they could say I failed to show up for work and could terminate my employment. I would lose my medical insurance, which I needed. I filed for retirement on September 30, 2004 at the State Public Employees Retirement System field office so I wouldn't have to face my employer. I sent a resignation letter to my chief, stating that I knew I would be risking my life in that old building if I returned.

After fourteen-and-a-half years of work and having an employer do this to me, was very hard. My disability was caused by the failure of my employer to provide a safe working environment. I could hardly breathe. There was no way I was going back to a sick building. By this time, I felt nothing but anger toward my employer and all the people involved in the lies. I felt betrayed by the people I trusted. However, I had to remember the word of GOD says:

Isaiah 54:17, *"No weapon formed against you will prosper, and every tongue that shall rise against thee in judgment thou shall condemn. This is the heritage of the servants of the Lord and their righteousness is of me, saith the Lord."*

The weapon had been formed, but no matter how long it was going to take, it would not prosper. At times, I was so frustrated that I didn't know what to believe. I was so sick at times and I felt so alone, but it was at those low points that God would intervene through a message by someone in song or ministry in a CD, DVD, or through Christian TV. I would feel the presence of Holy Spirit (the Comforter) who would comfort me and bring peace back into my spirit.

I had been a very active person all my life. I was a person who liked to stay busy. Living in the southern California region offered so much to do, and now I could no longer function normally. My whole world had stopped and made no sense. I remember one morning in September or October when I was dreaming that I was on an airplane. The plane was going very fast and couldn't stop. It was descending downward like it was coming in for a crash landing. Then I woke up. It was 6:30 a.m.. I felt the plane landed safely when I put my feet on the floor. I remember my life was so dark I didn't want to get out of bed, because I didn't know what tragedy I would be faced with that day. This dream represented my life before I got sick. I was busy and going very fast. Then everything began to come in for a crash landing with the injury. This is what happened to my life—it stopped and I landed.

Then on another occasion, I had a dream of being on a merry-go-round. I went around and around very fast and then all of a sudden, I got off the ride. I was standing on the outside looking at the world going around and around. People were in a frenzy going very fast, but headed nowhere. On the inside, I felt like a frightened little girl, not knowing what to make out of my life. I believe all of us as adults have either a little girl or a little boy inside.

I asked God, "Is this the end of my life? Am I getting ready to die, too? Or, would I make it to the other side of these horrific storms? I knew deep in my soul that I had an anchor, and that anchor was God. I was either going to trust him or believe all the negative circumstances that surrounded me. I had to trust God in the midst of the sickness and fear.

I felt like Job, in the Bible. He went through disaster after disaster. However, no matter how many horrific storms he went through, it covered a nine-month period. For me, it had been an eight-month period, but it felt like ten years.

The scripture says in St. Matthew 5:45, *"That ye may be the children of your Father which is in heaven: for he maketh his sun to rise on the evil and on the good, and sendeth rain on the just and on the unjust."*

I knew if I could get through one storm at a time, I would be okay. Every six weeks I was going through a major crisis. What had happened to my health from working in the sick building had become very hard for me to handle. It caused a domino effect in my life. I felt so violated and betrayed.

# PART 13

# THE END OF THE ROAD

November 1, 2004 was a turning point in my life where I just couldn't handle anything else. I had a scheduled appointment with my regular physician and my blood pressure was so high I was at a stroke level and didn't know it. I never in my life had blood pressure problems, but due to the grief, stress, and the twenty-pound weight gain from steroids, it hit me. The appointment was at 9:00 a.m., and my brother-in-law's funeral was at 11:00 a.m. I was feeling very down, which is not like me. I hadn't gone through depression since I became a Christian, but now I found myself feeling very sad. I had been going to my doctor for twelve years, and I never cried in front of him. I had always been a happy person, but that day I fell apart. He told me that in eight months I had gone through what most people don't go through in twenty years.

This was one of the days that seemed so "overwhelming." I took my eyes off God and looked at the circumstances, which frightened me. He talked to me for a long time, which was comforting. He let me know I hadn't gone crazy. I went through a year that most people would not go through in their entire life. I made a decision not to attend the funeral. I knew the family was grieving and I didn't want to be there and pass out, which would only make matters worst.

The same day my first retirement check arrived, after I had waited a month with no monies. It was $300 short; the State Public Employees Retirement System had made an error and I would get the $300 on December 1. Bureaucracy—they mess up and you have to wait. It took thirty days to correct their error. Now, I had no income from a job. I had no rental income from my tenants, since they were living on their last month's rent. I went home and went to sleep.

On November 10, 2004, I had another visit with my employer's doctor after my attorney had to get on my employer's attorney's case for not allowing their doctor to take pulmonary tests on me. When I saw their doctor, I just let him have it. I was fed up with all the anger, frustration, and games being played with my life. I asked him how he could deny me worker's comp considering that he never ran pulmonary tests to see what was happening internally. Then he said, "I will send you to the pulmonary clinic to have pulmonary tests done next week," which was November 18, 2004. He requested that I have breathing treatments after the first breathing tests, and then suggested that I retake the breathing tests again to see if the medication was helping. If I had not called my attorney, I would have never gotten another appointment to see their doctor again. They would have gotten away with denying my claim. I knew I should have had lung testing done two or three months prior to the November visit, but you have to fight for what is right. It's all about greed and money. They could care less about you. You're just another number or statistic.

My airways had a restriction or obstruction, which stopped 40 percent of air going into my lungs; this is why I was so weak and fatigued. I was still on steroids and taking breathing medicines that never worked in my system. Their doctor assured me I didn't have to come back. He would make his final report on what the pulmonary clinic said, and he did. That came out in my favor—my environment.

On November 18, 2004, I was taken to the same location for my pulmonary tests. The breathing treatment showed no change in my condition. I had an obstruction over my airways. I didn't find out his results until I had to go to my attorney's office for a deposition, which occurred in February 2005. Their doctor had ruled that my environment caused my injury—same as my doctor had said. It's so hard fighting when you're so ill, but you have to do it. It's a process you go through, and I knew I had to do it. It wasn't about money, because the governor had cut the worker's comp pay. It was about being violated and wronged. I was angry because I was a healthy person that just went to work and ended up with lung disease.

One morning about 12:30 a.m., I was watching Creation Scenes on Christian TV. There was a beautiful song called "Be Still" and the beautiful water scenes and trees were so soothing and comforting to me.

Psalm 46:10, *"Be still and know that I am God. I will be exalted among the heathen; I will be exalted in the earth."*

I had to be still, get quiet in my spirit, and wait for God to direct me.

# PART 14

# December 2004—Breaking Point

I had to make a decision in late September to put my rental property on the market to sell so I could survive. I told my tenants I was selling the property because I no longer worked due to my unexpected injury. I told them my sister, who is a real estate broker, would handle the sale of the property. Of course, they were very upset and didn't want to move. She served them the sixty-day notice that the house was going to be sold.

By December 2004, both homes I owned were behind in the mortgage payments, and thank God for my realtor sister and brother-in-law who loaned me the money to catch up with the payments on my rental property. I agreed to pay them back with the proceeds from the sale. Bill collectors were calling me like crazy. They wanted money, and they didn't want to hear what happened to me. They wanted their money, which I didn't have.

With the rental property, a servicing company handled the loan for the lender. The company was based in northern California. Loans were constantly being sold after people purchased them. With the hot real estate market in California, the lenders were using servicing companies. This service company would put my phone number on their automatic dialing system every day and they would hound you for money, even after you told them you didn't have it. I was so glad when the house was sold and the loan was paid off. My phone stopped ringing and I had peace again.

Back to my tenants; California law says you have to give tenants a sixty-day notice before you sell a rental property they are renting.

We abided by all the laws of the state. They were not very clean housekeepers, but they were nice people. When the "for sale" sign was posted in the middle of October, they became very upset. They didn't want me to sell my own property.

They signed a lease in the beginning naming the only persons that would be staying on the property, but then a few weeks later, the home became a hotel for all their family members. The other family members and friends moved in and they were not named on the lease. They could care less about me being sick. It was all about their family members having a place to stay.

I told my sister to give them first bid at the house to see if they could purchase it before it was sold. She even had a lender that would work with them, but they wouldn't call her. This was my house that my husband and I had purchased twelve years prior. We had worked hard keeping it in excellent condition, and I had a right to sell what I purchased.

My sister went through thirty potential buyers looking at my house in October and November 2004, which was during a hot sellers market in southern California. I had one of the top homes in the single family neighborhood of about 200 large, four-bedroom, two-story homes. It was a 2,000-square-foot home that sat on almost a half acre. The homes in my neighborhood were selling on an average of two days. Thanks to an honest realtor who showed the property, the outside was beautiful, but my tenants had trashed my beautiful home inside. That detoured potential buyers.

When I put the same house on the market to rent in June 2004, I had about twelve families that came by in a weekend. Everyone fell in love with the house and wanted to rent it.

This was my first and last time as a landlord. However, all things work out for good. In the latter part of 2004, the value of the property doubled.

On December 5, 2004, my tenants moved out, and I had a crew that went in the next day and spent a full day cleaning. My girlfriend hired a friend to haul the trash that was left in my home. He had a 20-foot truck and it was full of my tenant's trash—broken down couches, mattresses, etc.—unbelievable. I don't understand how people can be so "trashy" in such a short period of time. My house would have been lost if they had stayed any longer. I got my house back again, and by

December 6, 2004 when my sister and her husband went to see the house, they couldn't believe it. It was immaculate—the way I liked to keep my property. It was spotless.

I began to receive foreclosure notices on the condo because my other property had not sold. I was living on a retirement check. People were sending letters left and right saying that they could help me get out of financial problems with my house. After crying so much during the year of 2004, I didn't think I had any tears left to cry. I knew worry was faith in reverse, and God could not work on my behalf if I was not doing as the word says:

1 Peter 5:7, *"Casting all your cares upon him; for he careth for you."*

In my spirit, I knew deep inside the promise God had given me when I first started to fall behind financially.

I had a pity party with God, and remember that I cried to God when I saw the letter and said, "Now they're coming to take my house and I will be a homeless, sick bag lady. Plus, I can't breath. What do you want me to do, go and lie down in the middle of the main highway and let an eighteen-wheeler truck run over me?"

I was overwhelmed and at my total breaking point. I thought November was the end of me. I didn't think I could go through anything else, but I was wrong. Another crisis had come my way. Now, I know this is where God wanted me to realize how "fragile, powerless, and helpless I was as a human being." I had come to a point in my life where I had to let everything go and believe his word and trust him.

The scripture that kept coming to me in the word was,

**John 15:5**—*"For without me, you can do nothing."*

In my pity party, I told God I was a good wife, mother and a good employee. I didn't deserve all this evil that had come upon me. When I finished my pity party about thirty minutes later, I picked up my Bible and it flipped open to

Hebrews 6:15, *"And so, after he had patiently endured, he obtained the promise."*

I apologized to God for my pity party. I had patiently endured and now waited for the promise.

In the biblical story of Job, he was a good and honest man who had disaster on top of disaster that had come upon him. He lost his children, his cattle, his health, his finances, you name it; this poor man went through it. To put insult on injury, his wife told him to curse God and die and his three friends were no better.

Job 1:1, *"There was a man in the land of Uz, whose name was Job; and that man was a perfect and upright man and one that feareth God, and eschewed evil."*

But the Lord allowed Satan to come in knowing that Job would not stop trusting God after losing everything he had. Then the end of Job's story:

Job 42:12, *"So the Lord blessed the latter end of Job more than his beginnings."*

The Lord was giving me a promise like he gave Job, that my latter day would be better than the first.

The story of Job was an encouragement to me, knowing that if I would just hold on, things would eventually get better.

Back to the rental property—buyers were slow, coming through looking at the rental property because it was Christmas time and the real estate market is slow during the holidays. However, right after New Years 2005, a young couple with two little kids came through and the house sold and went into escrow. It sold in January and closed in February. My sister began to get calls and letters from people wanting to buy my house. There were checks from two other buyers sent to escrow as backups in case the young couple's loan didn't come through. I had three buyers in escrow. The house was immaculate again and now everyone who came through wanted to make an offer. The sign was taken down and the keypad removed from the house to stop realtors from showing the property. This was a major hurdle behind me now.

With the sale of the property, I was able to pay off all my bills, catch up with my condo and live on the rest, while waiting on my worker's compensation case to be settled.

I'm very grateful to God for his continual love, grace, and mercy towards me. I thank him for being an anchor of my soul and taking me through the galling winds to get to the other side of the storm, ALIVE. I know without a doubt, I would have never survived 2004 if I didn't have God in my life. This was my Hurricane Katrina.

# PART 15

# GRIEF SUPPORT FRIEND

Sometime during the month of October, I received a call from a friend who a few years prior had come to my other home for Monday night prayer. A minister friend told me this woman's daughter had been murdered in Los Angeles. I sent her a card via the minister and I put my new address and phone number on the card.

   We would spend time talking about the grief of losing loved ones over lunch at the $5.00 oriental food—all-you-can-eat buffet—in the high desert which was very good. We began to pray together on Mondays and we shared our losses over the next four months, encouraging one another. In order for healing to take place, you need to talk about your pain. I didn't think life could get any harder after the death of my dad in 2000. I was a daddy's girl, and I lost my dad and best friend. During 2004, in this season of our lives, we both had gone through horrific storms. We would laugh and cry. When one was up, the other was usually down, so we cheered each other up. We would pray and ask God that the killer would be found. In March 2007, our prayers were answered and a woman was arrested for her daughter's murder. She grew stronger, and was encouraging others, besides taking care of her elderly mother.

# PART 16

# LEGAL ENDURANCE

I had more pulmonary tests taken in January 2005 by my doctor. I had 10 percent more air going into my lungs in six months, but there were no other changes. There was still an obstruction over my airways.

In January 2005, I was taken off the steroids that I had been on for six months, along with the breathing medications—nothing had worked. There was nothing to treat me with—just rest and fresh air. I lived in the high desert where we have blue skies and clean air because of the elevation.

On February 3, 2005, my attorney wrote the city's worker's compensation attorney in an attempt to resolve the matter by an Agreed Medical Examiner (AME) whether my pulmonary injury came from the building or not. He would be amendable to (3) AMEs that were named. If any of these physicians were agreeable, he asked the other attorney to please arrange for an evaluation and send the joint letter for signature.

I had to let all fear go. I also had to forgive all the people who had wronged me. This was very hard. I was angry for being violated and no one cared. I was just another worker's comp case that they wanted to get rid of. It took months for me to forgive my employer because of their "lies and wickedness." I prayed and asked God to take unforgiveness out of my heart for these people, and not to allow me to become bitter.

If I had unforgiveness in my heart, I knew God would not forgive me and I could not receive my healing.

*I Peter 3:14, "But and if ye suffer for righteousness' sake, happy are ye: and be not afraid of their terror, neither be troubled."*

I received a letter on February 7, 2005 from my attorney's partner who had been periodically looking at my file for a possible third-party civil suit. This is when he advised me they would not be able to assist me in such an action, but that I had the right to consult with another law firm regarding the merits of my case. Lawyers do not want to deal with sick buildings; it's so hard to prove.

I was at a point now where I wondered what I should do. This was a step-by-step process with the worker's compensation case. The scripture says,

*II Timothy 2:3: "Thou therefore endure hardness, as a good soldier of Jesus Christ."*

The Bible was letting me know that as a born-again believer, I had enlisted in an army. As a soldier, I had to endure the hardness as a good soldier. Even after the disappointing news, I had to continue to go forward.

In February 2005, my employer's attorney had scheduled a deposition after two cancellations to be taken in my attorney's office on Valentine's Day, February 14, 2005. I drove over 200 miles round trip. Everything concerning my case had been done via mail, fax, and telephone calls to my attorney. That morning, I found out that my attorney had to go to court and one of the junior lawyers was going to sit in on the deposition. During the deposition, the city's attorney informed me that the deposition would take one hour, but it took two-and-a-half hours. Their attorney asked me questions and I began to expose what had transpired inside the old building, at which time he began to get angry. I felt he was not angry with me, but at the city, because he was hearing things he never heard about the old building.

Deuteronomy 33:29, *"Happy are thou, O Israel: who is like unto thee, O people saved by the Lord, the shield of thy help, and who is the sword of thy excellency! And thine enemies shall be found liars unto thee; and thou shall tread upon their high places."*

I thought I was the only employee who had gone forward with a worker's compensation claim against the "old building." My co-worker, who worked next to me after she was denied, never pursued it. I learned in May 2005 that a lieutenant had gotten sick and filed a claim in December 2004, claim number two. I heard a sworn employee I worked with had gotten sick from the building and filed a claim. This was claim number three. Therefore, by the beginning of 2005, there were three active claims. All the claims were denied, but they retained attorneys and pressed forward.

# PART 17

# HEALTH FOOD STORE—NATURAL HEALING

I had already been taking vitamins and herbs, so since none of the medications had worked, I went to a health food store and spoke with a nutritionist asking what natural vitamins, fruits and vegetables to take that would help my lungs. I was told to get antioxidants, Vitamins A, B complex, a lot of Cs, vitamins D, E, grape seed, and that I should drink green tea. In addition, I found out berries were good for lungs. I read two Christian books about natural remedies and natural foods to eat. I began to buy organic foods, that didn't have pesticides and I began to get stronger.

For years, my favorite aerobic exercise was walking, but after I took ill, I could not exercise for ten months. In April 2005, I brought a new treadmill and I was determined that I was going to exercise again by walking daily as I had previously done for many years. I was now faced with another medical illness—high blood pressure.

The soft tissue in my lungs and airways had been injured, so when I started my walking exercise I experienced pain (even though I was walking at a much slower pace) in the airway and lung area. I started crying. I was frustrated and angry because I couldn't do what I normally had done all my life—walk without experiencing chronic pain. I went back to the health food store and told the nutritionist. She said the body had been injured and when I started to exercise, it went literally into shock.

The nutritionist advised me to take more natural vitamin C (1500-2000 mg) daily before my walk, and it helped. I started walking four to five days at a slower pace. I started with one-half mile a day and then went to one mile after a few weeks. Then I walked two miles, and then two-and-a-half. I read an article from the Health Care Provider about a man who had been sick and lost weight by walking three miles a day to regain his health. I can't do a fast pace because I'm not healed yet, but I walk every morning on my treadmill. Before my injury, I would walk and pray before I went to work for several years. Now I was starting to do this again. It was the beginning of my healing process.

# PART 18

# THE MOVIE—ERIN BROCKOVICH

One day I was talking to a friend and the name Erin Brockovich came up. She asked me if I remembered the movie Julia Roberts was in called *Erin Brockovich*. It told the story about the people in Barstow, California who were getting sick. They found out there were contaminates in the water and they sued the company. I went to the video store and checked out the movie.

This was a true story where the people had become very sick by the contaminates and the cover-up by a company. This town was in California, and believe it or not, the city was about thirty minutes from my desert condo. I watched the movie over and over, and because Erin Brockovich worked for a law office, and after her own private investigation, she exposed the company. They gave her a very hard time, but she didn't give up. She kept on it until the truth came out and the company was taken to court and found negligent and liable.

I then went before the Lord in prayer. I said, "God, I don't understand. I'm out here all by myself. I filed a claim and my former employer is trying to discredit me by saying that my illness was not caused by the building. They have denied me from getting any compensation. What am I to do?"—as if God didn't already know about my woes? My answer was to "fight" my employer through the due process of law.

During 2005, I took on my own investigation like Erin Brockovich, since I couldn't get anyone to help. I went to the library and read up on the dangerous toxins. I searched on the Internet for any information on mold, since mold was found inside and outside of the building. On the web site of the Red Cross and the U.S. Government's EPA, I learned that molds release countless tiny, lightweight spores, which travel through the air. Mold spores primarily cause health problems when they are present in large numbers and people inhale many of them.

Molds will grow and multiply whenever conditions are right, and whenever sufficient moisture is available and organic material is present. The following are common sources of indoor moisture that may lead to mold problems. I listed only a few that would deal with an office building. The others were for a home—flooding, leaky roofs, plumbing leaks, overflow from sinks or sewers, damp basements or crawl spaces, and humidifiers.

The moisture was so high in the chief's office where I worked, and before I left in 2004, a humidifier was placed in his office. Several years before I began working in the office, I was told a new roof had been placed over the building during a rainstorm. Parts of the roof fell in the chief's office (no one was there) and it flooded. If mold was not properly taken care of in the walls, it could continue to make people sick. No one ever tested the walls. One sergeant had videos of the flooded second floor. This old police building had weathered many storms and this time, it was barely hanging on.

# PART 19

# My Faith in God Has Sustained Me

In the beginning of 2005, news was given to me that three more sworn officers had come forth with complaints to their union officials. A year later, other illnesses and claims against the old sick building came forth. All the money in the world could not pay for the pain and trauma that others and I had to go through with this employer. If they had admitted that the contractors errored and had gotten us help and compensation during the time I was ill, we wouldn't have had to get attorneys to fight for what was right.

When you're an active person and you get sick, your world falls apart. All you can do is take it slow. It's hard, but I know this was part of the healing process—taking life slow and resting.

On my refrigerator, I placed a small card that someone had given me a few years earlier with other cards and it read:

> *"Come unto me, all ye that labour and are heavy laden and I will give you rest. Signed JESUS."* Matthew 11:28.

So whenever I opened my refrigerator, I read the little card and smiled. I knew that JESUS loved me so much he wanted me to rest. When I felt anxious, I read the card and smiled. It made me slow down and rest.

After my retirement in 2004, it took a year for me to realize I didn't have to set the alarm for five o'clock in the morning. I didn't have to go to work anymore. I heard a lot of retirees say that it takes time to learn you don't have to get up so early after you stop working. So now, I get out of the bed a little later.

After months of being off and resting, I began to write down scriptures from the Bible. I repeated them out loud everyday as an action of my faith, believing God would hear and answer my prayers. When I read the promises in the scriptures daily during this horrific ordeal, it kept my hope and faith up. A few scriptures were:

Numbers 23:19, *"God is not a man that he should lie; neither the son of man, that he should repent hath he said, and shall he not do it? Or hath he spoken, and shall he not make it good?"*

I had to believe the Bible, the true and living word and not only read it, but believe what it said—that God was not a "liar." If you are given a promise in the Bible, then it will come to pass, **if you believe.**

2 Timothy 1:7, *For God has not given us the spirit of fear, but of power, and of love and of a sound mind.*

I spoke this scripture daily over my mind and I had to believe it in my heart because fear tried to grip my mind everyday. I had to say, "God has not given me a spirit of fear, but of power, love and a sound mind." From February 2005 to May 2005, I continued to rest, but I wasn't afraid like I had been. I was afraid of death and through the loss of several close loved ones, God had taught me this is a part of life.

I remembered when I was an eight-year-old girl I would go to bed and no one knew, but I would cry that God would not take my mommy and daddy away from me. I was afraid they would die and leave me, but God heard a child's prayer and he let my parents live a long and good life.

There were times when I thought my life was over due to the illness. I had to put closure on the three family deaths in 2004 and look forward. I knew that they had all accepted Christ, so I knew that it was all right. The financial crisis was over after all my bills were paid off, and my new home mortgage was caught up. All the bill collectors stopped calling and my house was very quiet now. My new grandbaby was doing fine. The only storm left to put closure on was my job and the worker's compensation case.

For each crisis, I felt like a swimmer. I would take a stroke and push one crisis behind me—one at a time and I kept looking forward. I knew if I looked at the circumstances I would drown, but if I focused my eyes forward, I would get through this crisis, too.

# PART 20

# RETIREMENT PARTY

On May 6, 2005, a couple of former co-workers, one in the police department and one in city hall, organized a "retirement luncheon" for me at my request. I had to abruptly leave a job of fourteen-and-a-half years and most people didn't know why I had left. I was so sick and angry when I left, it took seven months after my September 30, 2004 retirement date to realize that I could handle a small retirement luncheon with real friends and family. There were about forty to forty-five people in attendance at a nice restaurant located in another city at a new mall.

I told myself that I wouldn't let a few "wicked people" force me out of my job—totally disabled—and then be angry the rest of my life—or die bitter. I wanted to say good-bye to some of my friends whom I had worked with for almost fifteen years. I had a wonderful day and I received many cards, flowers, and gifts. So now, I was able to put closure on my career in this government and celebrate it with good people.

The interim police chief I worked with for five months, drove over 100 miles to attend my retirement party, which was very nice. One of my nieces flew in from northern California with her two daughters, and that was special. A few of my friends who had retired recently, showed up. I had friends attend who were from the police department and city hall, where I spent most of my years working.

Also, I was given a plaque which was presented to me by two beautiful people who worked for the local school district. I handled the police chief's entire booking on his calendar, so I was constantly setting up meetings with the alternative high school. Whenever they wanted to meet with the chief or have him come to speak, I would schedule them. I was just doing my job, not knowing I would be honored. The plaque said:

> **"Certification of Appreciation" The Alternative School of the Unified School District is proudly presented to Dorothy Ferrell for your endless assistance in all that we asked of you. Your immediate response and always-cheerful outlook was greatly appreciated. Signed the Director."**

This was so beautiful. For my entire working career, I learned to treat people the way I would want to be treated—with kindness and respect. I was thankful for this award and this beautiful good-bye.

# PART 21

# PERTINENT INFORMATION

After the deposition in February 2005, my case was given to the attorney who sat in on the deposition, but no one told me. I had some updated information to share with my attorneys, so I decided on May 7, 2005 to write a letter and forward that information. I sent the letter along with all the information. I was so excited. I knew this information was going to help me. I sent copies also to the two other attorneys in the office—my original attorney and the other attorney who was unable to file a civil suit. I wanted to let everyone know, "look what I have now."

In April 2005, I received a letter from my attorney for a medical appointment with a doctor closer to me, which was the day before my "retirement luncheon," on May 5, 2005. However, I didn't have good feelings about this appointment. This doctor I was to see was not on of the list of the three Agreed Medical Examiner's that both attorneys had agreed for me to see. I didn't say anything. I was excited about getting ready for my retirement party, but a few days before the party, I received a letter from my attorney stating that the appointment had been cancelled, which was fine for me.

On May 17, 2005, I received a letter from my attorney with the original deposition to read, sign, and send back. He said nothing about all the great information that I had sent. I woke up early on the morning of May 18, 2005. I was angry, frustrated, and discouraged. I was sick and tired of being sick and tired. I had lost my patience, and I was up at 6:30 a.m. in the morning—mad, and "typing away" on my computer. I composed a letter to my original attorney and I faxed it to him. Basically, I said I knew he had transferred my case and I got a letter from his partner saying he couldn't represent me in a third-party civil suit. I told him that I had been waiting since February 2005 for a response from the city's attorney to see an Agreed Medical Examiner. I had mailed information overnight express to all three attorneys on May 7, and by May 9, 2005, no one had responded.

I felt my case had fallen through the cracks after the transfer of my case to another attorney in the same office. Somehow, they had forgotten to send me a letter or call me saying my case was in the hands of another attorney in the law firm who handled "non-sworn personnel." I know attorneys have hundreds of cases, but I had lost my patience and I wanted to hear a good response from the paperwork, which I sent. As an injured worker, you don't feel good and going through the legal process is not easy. You try to be patient for a few months, and then you lose your patience because nothing is happening.

In my early morning letter, I said, "I'm very discouraged, frustrated and angered because I almost lost my life in the police department after inhaling toxins. I can't see how the laws of the state of California allow my employer and the contractor to expose a whole police department to deadly toxins and not be held accountable. Three months later, I'm still waiting for the city's attorney to schedule a doctor's appointment and for my attorneys to get any California Occupational Safety Health Administration (Cal/OSHA) reports on the building. I know the city's attorney is overloaded with cases, and I'm sure most of them are from the city in which I worked, but it shouldn't take this long to schedule a doctor's appointment. I know I have to see the Agreed Medical Examiner. I hope the city's attorney schedules me for an appointment in 2005."

"I know in law the 'proof of burden' has to be met. I was hoping the package I sent would help with the proof and not be ignored or just placed in my file."

"My request is if you would take my case back and if there is nothing the law can do regarding my case, close it out after the AME's evaluation, so I can close out this unpleasant chapter of my life. Thanks again for your help."

Then I started crying again. I'd had it. With the new worker's compensation laws, I felt I was a stranger in my own state, with no rights. The feeling that I felt was that the state of California worker's compensation laws were totally in the employer's favor, and that my employer could get away with not providing a safe work environment for me and jeopardize not only my life but also over 300 other innocent employees. The governor's overhaul cut injured workers' compensation way over the 50 percent mark, making it impossible for an injured worker and their family to survive.

A day or so later, I received from my attorney and the city's attorney a date to see the AME, which was June 9, 2005 in West Los Angeles.

Before the injury, I would host prayer breakfasts every quarter for three years at one of the local hotels. In 2004 after my injury, I had to cancel my entire ministry meetings, which was very hard. However, on June 4, 2005,—a year later—I was invited to speak at a Christian Women's Prayer Breakfast. I felt pretty good that day, so I went. When I came home from speaking that Saturday afternoon, there was a certified receipt in my mailbox. The mailman had tried to deliver it earlier, and I had to sign for it, but I wasn't home. I had no idea who it was from.

I had accepted a temporary work assignment in the desert for thirty days (this would be my first time trying to work since my injury) and I knew that Monday I had to go on this assignment. I wouldn't be home until after the post office closed. I left a note for my mail carrier, and I signed the certified receipt. I told him I was working temporarily and asked him to deliver it. After the thirty days was completed, I got so sick that it took me a month to feel better. I knew that my work career was over, and I didn't go back to work. I thought I was okay, but I didn't realize the full damage that had been done to my body.

On June 7, 2005, the letter was in my mailbox. It was from my attorney. It said that there might be a possible Serious and Willful allegation in my worker's compensation case. A Serious and Willful claim alleges extreme negligence on the part of your former employer as opposed to finding an outside "third-party" culpable for the harm. It is extremely difficult to win. Nonetheless, should such a claim be filed as part of your worker's compensation case, it would totally negate any third-party liability claim that you may want to pursue. Filing this would nullify any third-party civil case. I had to sign the letter and send it in by June 7, 2005. This was June 7, 2005 at 5:15 p.m., and the law office closed at 5:00 p.m.

I had a fax machine so I signed the letter, "**YES," I have nothing to lose."** I faxed it back, and then called and left voice mail messages for the front desk and my attorney's secretary's voicemails. It was accepted and the attorney did file the "Serious and Willful Violation" against my employer. On the acceptance letter I asked them to forgive me, I was very tired of the complete process and nothing seemed to be moving. The scripture for this time was:

> Psalms 70:1-3, *Make haste, O God to deliver me; make haste to help me, O Lord. Let them be ashamed and confounded that seek after my soul; let them be turned backward and put to confusion, that desire my hurt." Let them be turned back for a reward of their shame that say, aha, aha.*

I would have looked for another attorney to file a civil suit, but because of the information that was in the package,—I knew the pride and arrogance of my former employer—I knew something should be filed against them. They knew of the "recklessness" and still did not try to provide safe working conditions for their employees. This was negligence on their behalf.

On June 9, 2005, I went for my scheduled "AME" doctor's exam. It was a five-hour examination. I took so many lung tests that I was hurting in my airways and lungs afterwards. After the exam, I went home and rested.

On June 27, 2005, I went to a three-day Christian retreat about an hour-and-a-half from my home. When I returned, there was a voice message on my phone from my attorney asking me to call her. I went to the mailbox and there was a big brown envelope addressed to me from my attorneys. Inside was a twenty-two-page report from the Agreed Medical Examiner who had ruled in my favor. It said 100 percent of my illness was caused by my employment with the city government and I caused zero percent. The hard news for me to accept was that the diagnosis said I had 20 percent permanent lung damage. I was diagnosed with "Chronic Obstruction Pulmonary Disease." I never was a smoker. They prayed for me at the retreat and I was given a word that God was going to heal my body in his timing.

When I finally got to the page where it said "CAUSATION," it stated that I had no prior history of respiratory problems, asthma, or allergies that would have caused my lung illness. In other words, it was the building. When I read that section of the report, I broke down and wept with relief. I felt that weights had fallen off me. The battle had been long and hard. I had felt like a criminal for just going to work and inhaling dangerous poisons over my head.

My employer had not given me one dime to survive on since I had left. They denied all compensation due me as an injured worker. I was very thankful for having a job to work and pay the bills, but the job was a resource and God is my source. After eighteen months, and not one cent from my former employer, I survived. The scriptures I stood on were:

Psalm 25:3, *"Yea, let none that wait on thee be ashamed. Let them be ashamed which transgress without cause."*

Psalm 27:13-14, *"I had fainted, unless I had believed to see the goodness of the Lord in the land of the living. Wait on the Lord; be of good courage, and he shall strength thine heart; wait, I say, on the Lord."*

Psalm 69:3, *"I am weary of my crying; my throat is dried; mine eyes fail while I wait for my God."*

Psalm 69:6, *"Let not them that wait on thee O Lord God of hosts, be ashamed for my sake; let not those that seek thee be confounded for my sake, O God of Israel."*

During 2004 and 2005, I had lung testing at four pulmonary clinics, and saw several doctors, but God knew the final verdict regarding my injury. I was waiting for favor from God. On June 9, 2005, he gave me favor. The AME was the "referee" who made a final decision as to what had happened to me and where I was at medically. He ruled favorably, thanks be to the good Lord. Now here comes the judge.

# PART 22

# <u>Much Needed Vacation</u>

After all I had gone through, I wanted to go on a good vacation. When I sold my rental home in February 2005, I purchased a ticket for myself and my older sister to go on an Alaskan cruise with my pastor's ministry in July 2005. It was a seven-day cruise. I had not been on a cruise in twelve years and I knew this would be very therapeutic for me. I just wanted to get away from everything. Over the year, my older sister had always been a giver, and she lost her husband in 2004. I didn't know until after I had purchased the tickets that my niece would tell me my sister and my brother-in-law wanted to go to Alaska, too. However, he couldn't make it, but she went and we had a great time.

This was the most beautiful trip I had ever taken. All my problems had been cast in the Pacific Ocean. The day we traveled to the Hubbard Glaciers, I looked up at those glaciers and saw the handiwork of God. It was unbelievable.

I knew man could not build those glaciers, only God could have done that. These were glaciers from the ice age that stood hundreds of feet high (nothing but ice) and there were many seals that were at the base of the glaciers. Then I heard thunder and a piece of the ice fell into the ocean. It was so peaceful and serene. There were 1,800 passengers and 800 crewmembers on one boat. No one else was in sight—miles and miles of ocean. God gave me rest and peace.

Psalms: 94:12-13, *"Blessed is the man whom thou chasten, O Lord, and teachest him out of thy law. That thou mayest give him rest from the days of adversity, until the pit be digged for the wicked."*

PART 23

# Fight For a Court Date

In October 2005, my attorney sent me a copy of a "Supplemental Medical Report" which the AME wrote at the request of my employer's attorney. Neither the risk management department nor their attorney believed the building had made me sick, so they had the right to cross-examine the doctor. I had to continue being patient and wait on the Lord.

May 4, 2006 was set for a cross-examination date. I was totally shocked when I found this out. I had to wait eleven months after my AME exam for the attorney to cross-examine the doctor. My attorney contacted their attorney and told him there would be "severe prejudice for me." The AME doctor told them he would be happy to review any other medical reports, but the city had no other medical reports to submit to him. They kept sending him air quality reports written by an employee, and not a doctor.

I questioned the discrepancies with the report from the environmental company, and an e-mail from the safety officer pertaining to the air quality reports taken in July and August 2004—immediately after I was taken off work, totally disabled.

They said two different things pertaining to mold found in the building. The environmental company said that the mold did not cause any illnesses to the building occupants, but the safety officer's e-mail said "mold" was a suspect in triggering illnesses in the building.

I asked my attorney to seek a court date and I left the matter alone. The games seemed to never stop with my employer and their attorney.

You're not a person, you're a number, and they could care less about you. It's about money, lies and denial that anything ever happened in the old building.

# PART 24

# STRUGGLES WITH A FLAWED WORKER'S COMPENSATION SYSTEM

In early November 2005, I was sent a newspaper article from the Los Angeles Times by one of my prayer partners. The article was entitled, "Workers' Comp Changes Hurting Treatment, Medical Study Finds." It talked about how the governor's 2004 overhaul of a flawed worker's compensation system was having major problems.

The employers in the state of California had been dealing with worker's compensation fraud and extremely high worker's comp insurance premiums in the beginning of 2000. In order to try and fix a flawed system, the governor decided to overhaul the system in 2003 and 2004, which proved to be detrimental to injured workers and doctors. The doctors who were treating the injured workers throughout the state of California were locked into a system that is hostile to physicians and often harmful to the patients they served. The doctors said injured workers were being denied medical treatment. In addition, employers had become self-insuring carriers (they no longer hired an outside insurance carrier). This gave employers, like the one I worked for, the legal right now to deny honest claims, along with other insurance carriers. It became very vicious throughout the state.

After reading what California legislatures were saying about the complaints they had been receiving and what was happening to injured workers and doctors throughout the state, I decided to write a letter to my governor, senator, assembly member, and speaker of the California state legislature. I told them of my injury and the struggles I had been facing for almost a year and a half. I wrote the letter on November 8, 2005 and shared about the two major crises that happened with the renovation of the heating and air conditioning unit. I told them that it had made me and several of my co-workers ill and that the governor's new law gave my employer—who was self-insured—the right to deny honest worker's claims and treatment.

After thirty years working in administrative offices which included city and federal offices, along with the private sector, I saw many letters go out from executives I worked for. I learned whenever I couldn't get a problem solved or had a complaint and couldn't get anyone to help me, I would type a one-page or page-and-a-half letter, and send it to the three top people in charge of the business. Hopefully, one of the three would read the letter and respond. Guess what? It worked. Usually one of the three would write back; in my case, two wrote me back.

I received a letter in December from my state senator, whom apologized for the sufferings I had to go through with the system. He explained that the worker's compensation system overhaul was not meant to do harm to honest workers, and that the legislature was looking at reopening the law.

I received a letter from the California Labor Relations Department on behalf of the governor in response to my letter. This letter was full of bureaucratic red tape. The gentleman who wrote the letter went on about telling me to contact the Cal/OSHA (they had already been contacted). Everything I had already done, he was telling me to do it. Then finally, it ended with the California legislature reviewing the overhaul of 2004 and the permanently injured workers.

I wrote my state assembly member twice and neither he nor his aides responded. He couldn't write a simple letter back saying he was responding to my letter and they were reviewing the worker's compensation overhaul. However, he didn't do anything. That's why we as Americans need to consult God before we vote, and seek his face to know who should represent the people.

I never heard from the speaker of the assembly, either. I didn't vote for either one of these elected officials. Now I know why.

After being bombarded by constituents up and down the state of California, the legislature reopened the law in January 2006 in hopes of fine-tuning the wrong. The first item was revisiting the section about the permanent injured workers. The disability payments to permanent injured workers **was not supposed to be cut by over 50 percent.** This was a wrong that was done with the new law which cost injured people their jobs, families, homes, and most importantly, their lives.

In November or December 2005, I saw a newspaper article that named a group in the state, which dealt with representing injured workers. It stated that they worked with the state legislature to try and revisit the law and help work out the wrong.

In January 2006, through much prayer and fasting, the Lord gave me the name of an intercessor in the state capital through another intercessor from the east coast. I connected with this precious woman and she added my prayer request to her list. The California legislature revisited the law in 2006, and a review of the permanent disability was being reviewed first.

# PART 25

# COURT DATE FILING

In November 2005, my attorney notified me that a court date had been filed on my behalf, which requested a hearing date with the judge so the case could go forward due to the severe prejudice. I had not been given any aid or support since I left my job two years prior—just the sale of my personal rental property so I could survive during the process.

My attorney went to court in February 2006. The judge allowed the deposition of the AME and the attorney for the defense to go forth, but a May 23 date for a trial was set. This was a major victory for me.

# PART 26

# THE UNEXPECTED DEATH OF MY MOTHER

During the first week of January 2006, I went to a local Christian conference for a few days. My mother had been going back and forth to the hospital since about Thanksgiving for her stomach, but it was not life threatening. While I was at the conference, she was again taken to the emergency room. However, this time, a pneumonia outbreak had occurred at the hospital where my mother was and she caught pneumonia. My family called me, but God would not allow me to leave until Saturday, January 7, 2006. I had taken her picture to the conference and the prayer warriors were praying for her with all the other prayer requests twenty-four hours a day. I believed God would heal her, but he knew she was tired and it was her "sunset."

I arrived at the hospital with a friend who attended the conference with me. We anointed my mother with oil and prayed the prayer of faith over her. I was so sure that she would be healed, but God had other plans.

All my family members had been with mom all week, and I told her I would not leave her. I stayed all night at her bedside, holding her hand and comforting her. A peace came over my mother and all the swelling in her body left. At about 7:30 a.m. Sunday morning, my mom slipped into eternity. God had already strengthened me at the conference. I thought my life was coming together, and now this. We buried her next to my father a few days later. God had granted both of my parents longevity. She was in good health all her life until the last few weeks.

All her children, grandchildren, great grandchildren, sisters, and brothers were with her. About 300 family and friends came to the funeral chapel and the cemetery where she was buried.

# PART 27

# LETTING GO

When I went on the Alaskan cruise in 2005, I was at the Hubbard Glaciers and I remember talking to the Lord. I told him that I was casting every care and worry in the ocean, never to pick up again and I did, I thought. I had cast everything, but one thing, and the Lord brought it to my remembrance one morning about six months later when I was at home.

He told me you let go of everything except one thing—I want you to let the house go where I was living. I thought God meant for me not to worry, but trust him. I was working on a refinance on the property, which was due to close January 4, 2006. I had made it a year living on the remaining monies after paying off all the bills and catching up on the condo, but now the money was gone. The condo had fallen behind again because of lack of income and it was only two months before the settlement hearing.

When I returned after my mother's death on January 9, 2006, the escrow person had failed to process the paperwork in a timely manner. It fell through the cracks during the Christmas holidays, so the house had to be sold. The house sold for more than I owed on the loan, so I got my money in March 2006. During the two months of waiting on the closure of the property, I decided I had had enough of California and the wickedness. It was no longer the southern California I grew up in. I made plans to leave California after the May 23, 2006 worker's compensation hearing. Whichever way it went, I was leaving. My mind was made up, I consulted God, and I was given the green light to leave. After the house issue was settled, I stayed with a friend and her husband, and then I stayed with my son for a couple of weeks.

God was teaching me not to be self-dependent any longer, but to be God-dependent. After years of working and having my own homes, job, health, and family, I had to give it all up and trust God. This was very hard to do, but I had to obey, because of the call of God on my life. I knew in the end, whatever I had to give up, he would bless me with more.

# PART 28

# Court Hearing

After twenty-three long, agonizing months of waiting for my worker's compensation case to be resolved, the court date finally arrived. Before the hearing, the other side tried their last-minute ditch to stir up lies and make me look like the bad guy, but I continued to persevere with the case.

On May 23, 2006, my date to see the judge had arrived. I was still staying with my friend and her husband, which made it easier to commute to court. It wasn't as long of a drive as it would have been if I still lived in the desert.

I arrived at the state building that housed the Workers Compensation Court in the Van Nuys area of southern California. It looked like a mall of injured workers and lawyers—unbelievable. I went to sign in through the maze of people. It was overwhelming seeing so many injured workers and lawyers. After waiting about thirty minutes, my attorney arrived. After she signed in, she looked for my employer's worker's comp attorney. I waited in the large cafeteria area, which was located in the building in front of the offices of the Workers Comp Court.

My attorney came back and said their attorney wanted to work out a compromise before going to the judge. The compromise started at about 9:00 a.m., and I had to wait in the cafeteria area while the attorneys tried to work out a compromise settlement.

When I looked around at the sea of injured workers and lawyers, I saw so many angry faces. The governor's 2004 overhaul of the Worker's Compensation Program was detrimental to the injured workers and everyone involved. A couple of ladies told me that workers were crying while talking to their attorneys after finding out their settlements had resulted in close to nothing.

After working for over thirty years, I never thought I would see the day that honest injured workers would be treated so badly, but it was a reality. My attorney came down about three times asking me questions, and then she went back to the other attorney. Finally, just before lunch, they came up with a closed compromise settlement, which had to be approved by the judge after lunch.

After 1:30 p.m., the attorneys went before the judge and presented the compromise. The judge did not need to see me and signed the compromise. My attorney came down and congratulated me that it was over. It was as if weights fell off me. The nightmare was over. I fought tooth and nail to the end for the right to come forward. The fact of the matter was that I didn't give up. I prayed and trusted God's promises and I believed. Every promise in the Bible came true. It wasn't about money, because there wasn't a lot of money involved. It was the principle about what had happened and how it was handled. How could an employee go to work being healthy everyday, do a good job, and end up with lung disease by recklessness, and then be denied worker's comp payments? I had to give up everything I had worked for in a matter of months. They wanted to hush it up and they didn't want me to talk about it. But I wanted to do as Erin Brochovich did—talk about it and bring the truth out. I wanted to let others know about the dangers of old buildings and the dangers of inhaling poisonous toxins.

During the last year of this nightmare, I just wanted it over. I knew inside that I wanted to leave the state, and start a new life somewhere away from here.

Thirty days after the court hearing, I left my home state of California and moved to the Dallas, Texas area, where I completed this book. I attend my pastor's church every Sunday, and I am being strengthened spiritually and financially. I do ministry in the marketplace daily, telling people of the goodness of Jesus.

I started working temporarily this February 2007, and have been offered full-time positions with Fortune 100 and 200 companies in America.

I had another grandbaby born in March 2007, who was full-term and weighed 8 lbs. 6 oz. This is the first baby for my youngest daughter and her husband. I was shouting, excited, and happy. Everyone here in Texas asked me, "Is this your first grandchild?" I said no, it's number five. I was excited because God answered my prayer and let her be healthy and come home thirty hours after she was born. Out of five grandkids, two came home after they were born, and three ended up in neonatal intensive care for months—very sick and fighting for their little lives. This is why I shouted for joy with this birth. All the other grandchildren are doing fine, from the oldest to the youngest, thanks to the good Lord, and my kids are healthy and fine. I don't take life for granted. I thank God everyday for life and health of family, friends and myself. I don't worship material things, because it's just "stuff" that can be replaced, but lives cannot be replaced. So, enjoy your loved ones daily. Live one day at a time like it's your last day.

# PART 29

# LIGHT AT THE END OF THE TUNNEL

The California governor and legislature had been bombarded by thousands of letters and phone calls from angry injured workers, lawyers, doctors, and others, regarding the overhaul the governor instituted in 2004. In January 2006, the California legislature revisited the overhauled Workers Compensation System.

I wanted to share my story and I did, with a non-profit organization that works with the California legislature in the state capital in Sacramento. I saw their name in the newspaper article in November 2005, which I mentioned in Part 24 of this book. Their job has been to enact legislation that will help rebalance the California Workers Compensation System that has been fixed at the expense of the injured workers. My story was posted online at their web site, along with many other permanently injured workers in the state.

This group continues to do an outstanding job in fighting for the rights of the injured workers in the state. I am praying that God will answer the prayers of all those who have not only been injured on the job, but I pray for the lives destroyed because the system failed to pay permanent injured workers a fair salary to even buy food for their families.

There is a legislative bill already going before the governor to sign on behalf of increasing the permanent disability monies that were taken away. We ask God that he would send rightful leaders in the state of

California and in our nation who would stand up for what is right and moral.

The second thing is in June 2006 there was an article in the local newspaper in the city where I formerly worked. The article stated the city council was going to vote on an agreement to approve a new police building. They were trying to purchase the building right after I left, because the building we worked in was too old and sick. After I got sick, the police chief was working with the city council to purchase a building already built from the school district. It has taken two years to purchase, but I'm happy that the employees can have a new safe and healthy building to work in soon.

I quote from the newspaper article, "The police chief said should the agreement be approved, the city would be on its way to solving the problem of replacing the existing building—a problem it has been wrestling with for a number of years." One of the council members said, "Council members for a long time recognized the need for a new police building but financing was an obstacle. And a lieutenant said, "We desperately need that place. It's falling down around our ears."

That's good news for the workers who are still working at the police department. Finally, the police department is going to get a new building. Before it's over, hopefully the permanently injured workers in the state of California will be compensated fairly. I thank God for answered prayers that will help other employees in the city and throughout the state.

# PART 30

# <u>New Beginning</u>

Jeremiah 29:11, *"For I know the thoughts that I think toward you, saith the Lord, thoughts of peace, and not of evil, to give you an expected end."*

As I sit down at my computer and type the final chapter of this book almost three years after the nightmare, I know now that you can get through the most horrific storms in your life. There is a light at the end of the tunnel. It doesn't matter what storm you may be going through in your life. Always remember to trust God, even when you see no way out. As Christians, we walk by faith and not by sight.

When God told me to write a book about the horrific storm, I had to be sure it was God telling me this. It was very difficult. A couple of ministers were sent to confirm that I was to write a book about the ordeal. When I wrote the book, it was a healing process for me. I shared the grief, pain, and suffering I went through, all at the same time. In the end, it shows that God's word never fails. I wrote from my heart. I didn't know the first thing about writing a book, but I hope this book—from my heart to your heart—can encourage you to hold on and never give up.

One of the biggest challenges I faced was to forgive. It took months for me to forgive those who had wronged me. I understood that things in life happen to good people as well as bad, but I had to pray to

God to help me to forgive those who had fought so hard against me. Forgiveness is a key to healing. Once you forgive those who have wronged you, and release them, you can go forward to new and better things in life. If you don't forgive, it goes into a root of bitterness that can cause sickness in your body and I didn't want to be bitter.

I learned that through the storms you can become bitter or better. I chose to become better. I had to get free from the unforgiveness, anger, and rejection within me so I could move on with my life. I kept myself under a Bible-believing, spirit-filled church that not only teaches the Bible, but they believe it. Through modern technology, the DVDs and CDs I ordered through Christian ministry helped me to get to the other side of the storm.

Since my transition to Texas, I attend my Bishop's church here in the Dallas/Ft. Worth area. In 2007, I began working full-time again. I'm debt free and will be purchasing another condo soon. I now have a new beginning and I know that the best is yet to come. I have met so many beautiful people here in Texas. I made a choice to let go of the past and move forward. God has restored the dreams that he placed in my heart a few years ago, before the storms. I am going forth to walk into my destiny. The dreams were revelations that God dropped into my spirit. The Word says:

Job 23:10, *"But He knoweth the way that I take. When he hath tried me I shall come forth as gold.*

Job 42:12, *"So the Lord blessed the latter end of Job more than his beginnings."*

Hebrews 11:1, *"Now faith is the substance of things hoped for and the evidence of things not seen."*

Through it all, I have learned to take one day at a time and enjoy it to the fullness, as if it was my last. Love people and be happy.

# PART 31

# WORDS TO EMPLOYERS

If you are an employer and you have an old building, which you plan on doing an asbestos or hazardous materials abatement, or know someone in the process, please remove the people totally out of the building until it is completed. If the building is too old, look at ways to purchase a better building. Find reputable contractors with someone who can oversee the workers to make sure they take all the safety precautions— to not only protect themselves but the employees.

# PART 32

# Be Encouraged

I hope this book has encouraged you. Always remember, you are never alone during the darkest storms of your life when you have God in your life. He will be with you and see you through the other side of the crisis in your life, however horrific it may be. NEVER GIVE UP.

If you don't know God, and would like to accept him into your life, just repeat these words. It's very simple.

**Heavenly Father:**

I ask you to come into my life. I ask you to forgive me for all my sins. In the Bible, in Romans 10:9, 10 it says:

*"That if thou shalt confess with thy mouth the Lord Jesus, and shall believe in thine heart that God hath raised him from the dead, thou shalt be saved. For with the heart man believeth unto righteousness; and with the mouth confession is made unto salvation." AMEN.*

I pray God will guide you to a good church that teaches and believes the word of God.

May God bless you richly.

My name is Dorothy Ferrell. I am a pastor, bible teacher, motivational speaker, and now author. My former husband is deceased, and I am the mother of three adult children and six grandchildren.

I am the founder and president of the Run to the Water Ministries, a non-profit organization. In 2003, I was accepted as a member in The Potter's House International Pastoral Alliance (PHIPA), based in Dallas Texas.

Thirty years of my life was spent in the workforce as a senior administrative assistant in government, the private sector, and in corporate America. During my career, I had the responsibility of researching data to write business letters for my employers. This experience assisted me in writing my own motivational speeches and sermons. I never dreamed that one day I would write a book, but I have done just that.

I am forever grateful for God's grace and mercy in sustaining me through the horrific storms of life, and for also giving me the strength and courage to write this true story to share with others about the dangers of sick buildings and hazardous toxins.

Printed in the United States
95577LV00004B/481-486/A